Hello journal, my name is ______________________.
I am Pretty N' Purposed and ready to fill you up with amazing thoughts, plans and information!

I am fearfully and wonderfully created.
I am beautiful and I have Purpose!

VANIKA LEWIS

I am fearfully and wonderfully created.
I am beautiful and I have Purpose!

VANIKA LEWIS

I am fearfully and wonderfully created.
I am beautiful and I have Purpose!

VANIKA LEWIS

I am fearfully and wonderfully created.
I am beautiful and I have Purpose!

VANIKA LEWIS

I am fearfully and wonderfully created.
I am beautiful and I have Purpose!

VANIKA LEWIS

I am fearfully and wonderfully created.
I am beautiful and I have Purpose!

VANIKA LEWIS

I am fearfully and wonderfully created.
I am beautiful and I have Purpose!

VANIKA LEWIS

I am fearfully and wonderfully created.
I am beautiful and I have Purpose!

VANIKA LEWIS

I am fearfully and wonderfully created.
I am beautiful and I have Purpose!

VANIKA LEWIS

I am fearfully and wonderfully created.
I am beautiful and I have Purpose!

VANIKA LEWIS

I am fearfully and wonderfully created.
I am beautiful and I have Purpose!

VANIKA LEWIS

I am fearfully and wonderfully created.
I am beautiful and I have Purpose!

VANIKA LEWIS

I am fearfully and wonderfully created.
I am beautiful and I have Purpose!

VANIKA LEWIS

I am fearfully and wonderfully created.
I am beautiful and I have Purpose!

VANIKA LEWIS

I am fearfully and wonderfully created.
I am beautiful and I have Purpose!

VANIKA LEWIS

I am fearfully and wonderfully created.
I am beautiful and I have Purpose!

VANIKA LEWIS

I am fearfully and wonderfully created.
I am beautiful and I have Purpose!

VANIKA LEWIS

I am fearfully and wonderfully created.
I am beautiful and I have Purpose!

VANIKA LEWIS

I am fearfully and wonderfully created.
I am beautiful and I have Purpose!

VANIKA LEWIS

I am fearfully and wonderfully created.
I am beautiful and I have Purpose!

VANIKA LEWIS

I am fearfully and wonderfully created.
I am beautiful and I have Purpose!

VANIKA LEWIS

I am fearfully and wonderfully created.
I am beautiful and I have Purpose!

VANIKA LEWIS

I am fearfully and wonderfully created.
I am beautiful and I have Purpose!

VANIKA LEWIS

I am fearfully and wonderfully created.
I am beautiful and I have Purpose!

VANIKA LEWIS

I am fearfully and wonderfully created.
I am beautiful and I have Purpose!

VANIKA LEWIS

I am fearfully and wonderfully created.
I am beautiful and I have Purpose!

VANIKA LEWIS

I am fearfully and wonderfully created. I am beautiful and I have Purpose!

VANIKA LEWIS

I am fearfully and wonderfully created.
I am beautiful and I have Purpose!

VANIKA LEWIS

I am fearfully and wonderfully created.
I am beautiful and I have Purpose!

VANIKA LEWIS

I am fearfully and wonderfully created.
I am beautiful and I have Purpose!

VANIKA LEWIS

I am fearfully and wonderfully created.
I am beautiful and I have Purpose!

VANIKA LEWIS

I am fearfully and wonderfully created.
I am beautiful and I have Purpose!

VANIKA LEWIS

I am fearfully and wonderfully created.
I am beautiful and I have Purpose!

VANIKA LEWIS

I am fearfully and wonderfully created.
I am beautiful and I have Purpose!

VANIKA LEWIS

I am fearfully and wonderfully created.
I am beautiful and I have Purpose!

VANIKA LEWIS

I am fearfully and wonderfully created.
I am beautiful and I have Purpose!

VANIKA LEWIS

I am fearfully and wonderfully created.
I am beautiful and I have Purpose!

VANIKA LEWIS

I am fearfully and wonderfully created.
I am beautiful and I have Purpose!

VANIKA LEWIS

I am fearfully and wonderfully created.
I am beautiful and I have Purpose!

VANIKA LEWIS

I am fearfully and wonderfully created.
I am beautiful and I have Purpose!

VANIKA LEWIS

I am fearfully and wonderfully created.
I am beautiful and I have Purpose!

VANIKA LEWIS

I am fearfully and wonderfully created.
I am beautiful and I have Purpose!

VANIKA LEWIS

I am fearfully and wonderfully created.
I am beautiful and I have Purpose!

VANIKA LEWIS

I am fearfully and wonderfully created.
I am beautiful and I have Purpose!

VANIKA LEWIS

I am fearfully and wonderfully created.
I am beautiful and I have Purpose!

VANIKA LEWIS

I am fearfully and wonderfully created.
I am beautiful and I have Purpose!

VANIKA LEWIS

I am fearfully and wonderfully created.
I am beautiful and I have Purpose!

VANIKA LEWIS

I am fearfully and wonderfully created.
I am beautiful and I have Purpose!

VANIKA LEWIS

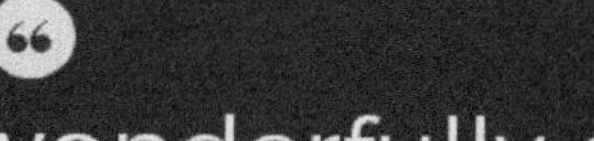

I am fearfully and wonderfully created.
I am beautiful and I have Purpose!

VANIKA LEWIS

For I know the plans I have for you,"
declares the Lord, "plans to prosper you
and not to harm you, plans to give you
hope and a future.

JEREMIAH 29:11

Pretty And Purposed, LLC
IG: @prettynpurposed

Owned and managed by Vanika Lewis
www.vanikalewis.com
@ladyv_lewis

www.ingramcontent.com/pod-product-compliance
Ingram Content Group UK Ltd.
Pitfield, Milton Keynes, MK11 3LW, UK
UKHW051135260726
13967UKWH00010B/3056

9 780359 119509